Athena

Gracie Gardner

methuen | drama

LONDON • NEW YORK • OXFORD • NEW DELHI • SYDNEY

METHUEN DRAMA
Bloomsbury Publishing Plc
50 Bedford Square, London, WC1B 3DP, UK
1385 Broadway, New York, NY 10018, USA
29 Earlsfort Terrace, Dublin 2, Ireland

BLOOMSBURY, METHUEN DRAMA and the Methuen
Drama logo are trademarks of Bloomsbury Publishing Plc

First published in Great Britain 2021

Cover photo by Camilla Greenwell

Cover artwork by Guy J Sanders

A catalogue record for this book is available from the British Library.

A catalog record for this book is available from the Library of Congress.

ISBN: PB: 978-1-3503-0060-6
ePDF: 978-1-3503-0061-3
eBook: 978-1-3503-0062-0

Series: Modern Plays

Typeset by Mark Heslington Ltd, Scarborough, North Yorkshire

To find out more about our authors and books visit
www.bloomsbury.com and sign up for our newsletters.

Athena

Written by Gracie Gardner

CAST

Athena	**Millicent Wong**
Mary Wallace	**Grace Saif**
Jamie	**Amaia Aguinaga**

TEAM

Writer	**Gracie Gardner**
Director	**Grace Gummer**
Designer	**Ingrid Hu**
Sound Designer	**Esther Kehinde Ajayi**
Lighting Designer	**Marty Langthorne**
Movement Director	**Yami Löfvenberg**
Fight Director	**Claire Llewellyn**
Casting Director	**Naomi Downham**
Assistant Director	**Amber Evans**
Production Manager	**Tom Wilson**
Company Stage Manager	**Devika Ramcharan**
Assistant Stage Manager	**Sussan Sanii**

This version of *Athena* was first produced by The Yard Theatre, 4 October 2021, as part of the NT Women of Tomorrow Directors Award.

The NT Women of Tomorrow Directors Award is supported by the CHANEL Fund for Women in the Arts and Culture.

Athena was commissioned by and received its world premiere with The Hearth (Emma Miller and Julia Greer, Co-Artistic Directors) at JACK in Brooklyn, New York, on February 16, 2018.

This production of Athena was developed with support from Arts Council England, National Theatre, Theatre Together & Golsoncott Foundation.

Millicent Wong | ATHENA

Millicent trained at The Royal Central School of Speech & Drama.

Theatre credits include: *After Life* (National Theatre), *The Living Newspaper 6* (Royal Court), *The Doctor* (The Adelaide Festival), *The Lion, The Witch and The Wardrobe* (Bridge Theatre), *The King of Hell's Palace* (Hampstead Theatre) and *Pah-La* (The Royal Court).

Television credits include: *Silent Witness* (BBC), *Annika* (Alibi), *Dracula* (Netflix).

Grace Saif | MARY WALLACE

Grace Saif trained at the Royal Academy of Dramatic Art.

Theatre credits include: *The Prime of Miss Jean Brodie* (Donmar Warehouse), *Saint George and The Dragon* (National Theatre), *Mary Stuart* (Almeida), *Antony & Cleopatra* (Gate Theatre).

Television credits include: *Doctors* (BBC), *13 Reasons Why* Seasons 3 & 4 (Netflix).

Amaia Aguinaga | JAMIE

Amaia graduated from The Brit School in 2018.

Theatre credits include: *What Was Left* (Southwark Playhouse).

Film and television credits include: *Us* (BBC), *Sulphur & White* (AMG International films, EMU Films, Stage 5 Films).

Amaia was also part of the Andrew LLoyd Webber Foundation Theatre Bridge Company and Frantic Assembly's First Ignition for Women.

Gracie Gardner | Writer

Gracie Gardner is an American playwright.

Theatre credits include: *Decoys* (McKnight National Residency), *Pussy Sludge* (Relentless Award, Theatertreffen Stückemarkt), *I'm Revolting* (Atlantic Theater Company Claire Tow Fellowship), *Hate Baby* (James Stevenson Prize), *Panopticon* (Clubbed Thumb).

Work in development with: New Dramatists, Ars Nova Play Group, Manhattan Theater Club, SPACE on Ryder Farm, Ensemble Studio Theater's Youngblood, The Old Vic, The New Group, Two River Theater, Williamstown Theater Festival.

Work published by: Samuel French, Table Work Press, S. Fischer, *Cincinnati Review*.

Grace Gummer | Director

Grace Gummer is the first recipient of the NT Women of Tomorrow Directors Award, as part of a partnership with the CHANEL Fund for Women in the Arts and Culture and inaugural venue partner The Yard Theatre. Grace was selected from over 160 applicants by the panel, which included representatives from the National Theatre and The Yard.

Grace worked as Resident Assistant Director at The Yard Theatre on *LINES* by Pamela Carter, *RE:Home* by Cressida Brown, and Alexander Zeldin's production of *Beyond Caring* (transferred to the Shed at the National Theatre in 2015). Grace was also previously trainee director at the Royal Court in 2016–2017, and assisted on *Anatomy of a Suicide, Road, Victory Condition, Gun Dog* and *Glass. Kill. Bluebeard. Imp.* Grace was Literary Associate at the Royal Court in 2019.

Directing credits include: *Reality* (Royal Court and RWCMD co-commission in Cardiff, and at the Gate Theatre), *Roman Candle* (Theatre 503, toured Manchester, Edinburgh and Burnley), *Butter* (the Vaults, won an Origins Award for Outstanding New Work), *Germ Free Adolescent* (Bunker Theatre).

Ingrid Hu | Designer

Ingrid Hu is a scenographer, designer and artist working in theatre and multidisciplinary design. With a focus on materiality, contextual and conceptual thinking, she creates spaces and environments that are alive and empowered to co-author and respond to contemporary narratives. She joined the award-winning Heatherwick Studio in 2002 and has worked on a wide range of projects including the UK Pavilion for the 2010 World Expo, for which she received a D&AD award in Spatial Design.

Theatre credits include: *The Global Playground* (Manchester International Festival/Theatre Rites, Great Northern Warehouse, Manchester), *Chotto Xenos* (Akram Khan Company, world tour), *The Slightly Annoying Elephant* (Little Angel Theatre, London, UK), *Light /Dark* (Uppsala, Sweden), *Curiouser* (UK/Norway tour), *A Kettle Of Fish* (The Yard Theatre, London, UK), *Zeraffa Giraffa* (Little Angel Theatre and Clapham Omnibus Theatre, London, UK), *We Raise Our Hands In The Sanctuary* (The Albany, London, UK), *Music Impossible* (LSO St Luke's & St Paul's Church, London, UK), *Hong Kong Impressions* (Yuen Long Theatre, Hong Kong), *1908 Body and Soul* (Jacksons Lane Theatre, London, UK), *You May!* (The Place, Arnolfini, UK; Onassis Culture Centre, Greece), *The Van Man* (UK national tour), *The Girl Who...* (Spitalfields Market & The Rag Factory, London, UK), *THEATRE OF THE VISCERA* (La Nef Manufacture d'utopies, France), *The Bell Ringer* (Dilston Grove, London, UK), *Medea, The Foreigner* (Bridewell Theatre, London, UK), *On the Cusp* (Camden Roundhouse studio, UK).

Esther Kehinde Ajayi | Sound Designer

Esther Kehinde Ajayi is a creative sound designer based in London and Berlin. Esther's practice explores the relationships between sound, narrative and our innate human need for love, connection and the fulfilment of our desires.

Marty Langthorne | Lighting Designer

Marty Langthorne is a lighting designer for Theatre, Performance and Installation.

Some recent work includes: *The Philharmonia Orchestra* (BAC and Royal Festival Hall), *My Body My Archive* (Tate Modern), *The Candle Project* (Abigail Conway), *The Adventures of Curious Ganz* (Silent Tide, Little Angel Theatre), *Museum of Water* (Amy Sharrocks), *Re-member Me*, *Camera Lucida*, *Blackouts*, *Lost in Trans* (Dickie Beau), *Party Skills for the End of the World* (Nigel & Louise, Shunt), *The Assembly of Animals* (Tim Spooner), *Credible Likable Superstar Rolemodel* (Bryony Kimmings), *The Iron Man* (Matthew Robins), *Svatantrya* (Anoushka Shankar), *Vincent River* (Park Theatre), *Rat Rose Bird & Sulphur* (Sheila Ghelani), *Lines & Made Visible* (The Yard Theatre), *Fat Blokes, Class & The Worst of Scottee* (Scottee), *Our True Feelings*, *Choreography of an Argument Around a Table*, *Tug* (Dog Kennel Hill Project/The Yard Theatre), *Plastic Soul* (Seke Chimutengwende/The Yard Theatre), *Longing Lasts Longer* (Penny Arcade).

As part of the Duckie collective, he has designed many of their theatrical club events.

As a light artist, he creates installations investigating human response to colour in the natural world.

Yami Löfvenberg | Movement Director

Yami Löfvenberg is a multidisciplinary artist and director working in the intersection of movement, theatre and cross arts. Between making theatre and her own work, Yami mentors, educates and delivers workshops nationally and internationally. Yami currently is the lecturer on the first ever Hip-Hop module at Trinity Laban Dance Conservatoire. Yami is a British Council and Arts Council England recipient, Howard Davies Emerging Directors Grant Recipient, One Dance UK DAD Trailblazer Fellow, Marion North Recipient, and a Talawa Make Artist. She was on the creative choreographic team for the 2012 Olympics Opening Ceremony and is a member of performance collective Hot Brown Honey. Yami has a collaborative company called Passion & Purpose that focuses on dance management, creative projects and artist progression.

Movement Director credits include: *Notes on Grief* (Manchester International Festival), *Rare Earth Mettle & Living Newspaper* (Royal Court), *Fuck You Pay Me* (The Bunker Theatre), *Breakin' Convention* (Sadler's Wells), *Talawa TYPT* (Hackney Showroom), *Boat* (Battersea Arts Centre). Theatre Director credits include: *Fierce Flow*

(Hippodrome Birmingham), *Kind of Woman* (Camden People's Theatre), *Afroabelhas* (Roundhouse/British Council/ Tempo Festival (Brazil).

Assistant Director/Choreographer credits include: *Hive City Legacy* (Roundhouse, Home, Millennium).

Claire Llewellyn | Fight Director

Claire is an Associate Fight Director with Rc-Annie Ltd.

Recent Fight Direction credits: *Carmen* (OperaNorth), *Don Giovanni* (Nevill Holt Opera), *Witness for the Prosecution* (London County Hall), *The Prince of Egypt* (Dominion Theatre, Associate FD), *The Process* (Bunker Theatre), *Ages of the Moon* (The Vaults), *Frankenstein* (NYT Rep), *Whoddunit* (Park Theatre), *Wait Until Dark* (Frinton Summer Theatre), *King Lear* (Progress Theatre), *Love of the Nightingale* (Salisbury Playhouse), *Romeo and Juliet* (China Plate Theatre), *Hansel and Gretel* (Rose Theatre Kingston), *Witness for the Prosecution* (County Hall as Associate Fight Director), *The Paradise Circus* (The Playground Theatre), *Sense and Sensibility* (Wokingham Players), *Macbeth* (Merely Players), *Function* (National Youth Theatre of Great Britain), *When They Go Low* (National Connections), *La Tragedie de Carmen* (Royal Academy of Music), *The Host*, *Zigger Zagger*, *Blue Stocking*, *Bitches* (National Youth Theatre), *Cluedo Killing Club* (Arcola Theatre), *A Flea in her Ear*, *Things we do for Love* (Wolkingham Theatre), *Bitched* (Tristan Bates), *Twist* (Theatre Centre), *Boom* (Theatre 503), *Othello*, *King Lear*, *Much Ado About Nothing* (Scaffold State), *Peter Pan "The Never Ending Story"* (Al Raha Beach Theatre, Abu Dhabi), *Not a Game for Boys* (King's Head Theatre), *Macbeth* (Greenwich Theatre), *The White Devil* (Eton College), *Jack and the Beanstalk* (Park Theatre).

Fight Assistant credits: *4.48 Psychosis* (Royal Opera House/Lyric Hammersmith), *Don Giovanni* (Royal Academy of Music), *Deathtrap* (TMO Productions and Salisbury Playhouse), *Wait Until Dark* (Original Theatre Company), *Red Velvet* (The Tricycle Theatre and Motion Pictures Arthur and Merlin and Howl).

Naomi Downham | Casting Director

Naomi is currently Senior Casting Assistant at The Royal National Theatre, having started her career as a Junior Agent at Lou Coulson Associates.

She works across all three theatres on the South Bank as part of the NT Casting Department and her most recent co-credits include: *The Normal Heart* (Olivier Theatre, dir. Dominic Cooke), *Death of England: Face to Face* (Film, dir. Clint Dyer), *The Ocean at The End of the Lane* (Dorfman Theatre, dir. Katy Rudd).

Amber Evans | Assistant Director

Amber is a theatre maker and performer who trained at the Royal Central School of Speech and Drama.

As a freelance artist, she has worked with Disney, TALAWA, Eastside Educational Trust and The Old Vic.

Amber worked as a facilitator for Yard Young Artists at The Yard Theatre, and is excited to be working at The Yard again.

Credit as Assistant Director; *EVERYTHING* (Company Three).

Tom Wilson | Production Manager

Tom is a Production Manager who works across digital and real-life spaces. He graduated from the Recording Arts degree programme at SAE Institute, and accidentally ended up working in theatre after supporting himself through his studies with occasional work in venues across London.

As a Production Manager, he helps facilitate the work of Brian Lobel, FK Alexander, Martin O'Brien, Daniel Oliver & Frauke Requardt, The Wellcome Collection, Something To Aim For, and The Sick Of The Fringe. He is also an occasional Sound Designer, specialising in site-specific and participatory theatre.

Tom is a member of the technical team in the Drama Department at Queen Mary University London, as well as being an associate teacher in the Technical Theatre department at RADA, and a student mentor at ALRA.

Devika Ramcharan | Company Stage Manager

Devika is a Stage Manager based in London and holds a BA in Theatre Practice: Stage Management from Royal Central School of Speech and Drama.

Credits as Company/Stage Manager on the Book include: *Extinct* (Theatre Royal Stratford East), *Mephisto* (The Gate), *The Realistic Joneses*, *Blue Door* (Ustinov at TRB), and *Kettle of Fish* (The Yard Theatre).

Sussan Sanii | Assistant Stage Manager

Sussan is a stage manager from Florence, Italy, of American and Iranian heritage.

As a member of NYT Sussan worked as Assistant Stage Manager on *DNA* (Southwark Playhouse) and *Macbeth* (Garrick Theatre).

Sussan has been part of the Stage Management team at Italia Conti Academy for 4 years. Assistant Stage Manager credits at Italia Conti include: *Revolt. She Said. Revolt Again*, *Consent* and *The Pride*.

Other Stage Manager credits include: *The Octopus* (King's Head Theatre, Playmill Festival).

Athena Supporter Credits

This production of *Athena* was developed with support from Arts Council England, National Theatre, Theatre Together & Golsoncott Foundation.

The NT Women of Tomorrow Directors Award is supported by the CHANEL Fund for Women in the Arts and Culture.

CHANEL FUND FOR WOMEN
IN THE ARTS AND CULTURE

The Yard Theatre

"The future has arrived in Hackney Wick in the form of The Yard" –
Lyn Gardner, *The Guardian*

The Yard is a theatre and music venue in a converted warehouse in
Hackney Wick.

The Yard was founded by Artistic Director Jay Miller in 2011, with
support from Tarek Iskander, Sasha Milavic Davies and Alex Rennie
and a group of 50 volunteers. They worked with architectural firm
Practice Architecture to convert a disused warehouse into a theatre
and bar.

The Yard is at the centre of its community, reaching thousands of
local people every year through programmes in local schools and in
the community centres they run: Hub67 in Hackney Wick and The
Hall in East Village. The Yard runs creative projects for young people
aged 4–19 years to make work for their stage, and offer regular
activities and resources for local people.

The Yard is also one of London's most exciting venues for
experiencing music, welcoming parties by and for under-
represented groups in London's music scene, as well as hosting
internationally renowned DJs and promoters every weekend.

Since 2011 The Yard's work has been seen by hundreds of thousands
of people and shows have have transferred to the National Theatre,
been turned into television series and toured the UK.

Recent productions include:

Dirty Crusty written by Clare Barron, directed by Jay Miller
★★★★★ *Evening Standard*

Armadillo written by Sarah Kosar, directed by Sara Joyce
★★★★ *The Guardian*

The Crucible written by Arthur Miller, directed by Jay Miller
★★★★★ *Evening Standard*

A New and Better You written by Joe Harbot, directed by Cheryl Gallacher ★★★★ *The Guardian*

Buggy Baby written by Josh Azouz, directed by Ned Bennett ★★★★★ *WhatsOnStage*

This Beautiful Future written by Rita Kalnejais, directed by Jay Miller ★★★★★ *The Stage*

Removal Men written by M. J. Harding, with Jay Miller ★★★★ *Time Out*

LINES written by Pamela Carter, directed by Jay Miller ★★★★ *Time Out*

The Mikvah Project written by Josh Azouz, directed by Jay Miller ★★★★ *Time Out*

Beyond Caring by Alexander Zeldin ★★★★ *The Guardian*

Artistic Director	Jay Miller
Executive Director	Sam Hansford
Associate Director	Cheryl Gallacher
Associate Director	Anthony Simpson-Pike
Senior Producer	Ashleigh Wheeler
Theatre Producer	Lara Tysseling
Theatre Assistant	Peyton Lee
Local Producer	Katherine Igoe-Ewer
Local Coordinator	Holly Campbell-Smith
Music & Events Producer	Anjali Prashar-Savoie
Music & Events Assistant Producer	Marissa Malik
Operations Manager	Felix Yoosefinejad
Development Manager (Maternity Cover)	Gareth Cutter
Development Officer	Faiza Abdulkadir
Finance & HR Manager	Susie Italiano
Finance & HR Officer	Kellie Grogan
Communications Officer	Kia Noakes
Technical Manager	James Dawson
Production Coordinator	Esmé Lewis-Gartside
Bar Manager	Max Hesmondhalgh
Front of House Manager	Grace Ogunnusi
Cleaner	Kay Adedeji
Kitchen Resident	Seif Abdel Salam from Taheena

Greg Delaney
Ian & Janet Edmondson
Pam & Peter Hansford
Jack Haynes
Nick Hytner
Alex Ingram
Melanie Johnson
Joanna Kennedy
Lauren McLeod
Ben Rogers
Robin Saphra
Peter Snook
Nick Starr
Clive & Sally Sherling
Anna Vaughan & Dan Fletcher
Adam Tyndall
Archie Ward
Carolyn Ward
Emily Warner
Garry Watts
Hyman Wolanski
Gabriel Vogt

And all our supporters who prefer to remain anonymous

Corporate Supporters

Bristows LLP

Takero Shimazaki Architects

Thanks

Thank you to everyone who helped us make *Athena*. We couldn't
have done it without you.

The team who made the show would like to thank:

Camilla Greenwell, Guy J. Sanders, Katy De Main, Nick Flintoff and
Stewart Pringle at National Theatre New Work Department, Roger
at Digital-4.co.uk

Athena

Characters

Mary Wallace

Athena

Jamie

We're at the Fencers Club. It's fall. It's a regional tournament.
Athena *attacks* **Mary Wallace**, *hits. Buzzer and light to* **Athena**.
Athena *screams. It's a howling, unearthly, whatthefuck kinda
scream.* **Mary Wallace** *collapses. Bent over, hands on knees at first,
she begins to cry. Then, falling to her knees, the weeping begins.*
Mary Wallace *weeps like she's retching, like she's purging, like
nothing else matters. On all fours,* **Mary Wallace** *weeps with her
whole body, like her son has died at sea, like her life is over, like she
knows she has something left but doesn't know what it is. It's loud,
rhythmic, heaving sobs. It lasts. And* **Athena** *is still there, trying to
get* **Mary Wallace** *to shake her hand.* **Athena** *watches* **Mary
Wallace** *weep and weep and weep.* **Mary Wallace** *removes her
mask and wipes away a mass of snot and drool.*

Athena   Good bout.

Mary Wallace (*getting it together*)   Thank you.

Athena   Are those your parents?

Mary Wallace   Yeah.

Athena   Look, they brought you flowers.

Mary Wallace *loses it again.*

I get emotional too. Sometimes, after I lose? I'll bump into
a random person on the street, on purpose. And I won't
say sorry.

Mary Wallace   That's nice of you to say.

Athena   You must really care.

Mary Wallace   I do.

Athena   I do too. We should train for Nationals together.

Mary Wallace   I don't think that's a good idea.

Athena   We're well matched.

Mary Wallace   You just beat me in the toughest bout I've
ever fenced so like . . . I'm feeling a little down.

Athena   Exactly, it was a tough bout. We'll get better together!

Mary Wallace   But you just won. You're better than I am.

Athena   That could have gone a different way. How are you seeded?

Mary Wallace   In state? Um, this morning I was fifty-four.

Athena   I was fifty-five.

Mary Wallace   Well . . . Now *you're* fifty-four.

Athena   So what? If we train together, we improve together, because we're neck and neck. Forty, forty-one. Twenty-six, twenty-seven. You know? Number one!

Mary Wallace   Number two.

Athena   I was having fun! This was a fun match for me. Wasn't it for you? You were having fun.

Mary Wallace   I was not.

Athena   Oh, come on. Sometimes I forget that I *like doing this*.

Mary Wallace   I'm a sore loser. I'm not going to be able to admit there was fun involved.

Athena   You would be a sore loser if you didn't practice with me just because you lost.

Mary Wallace   I train at home.

Athena   With what?

Mary Wallace   My wall.

Athena   That's very impressive that you're this good with just you and your wall.

Mary Wallace (*she knows it but she wants to hear it straight*)   You think I'm good?

Athena (*factually*)   You're very good.

Mary Wallace   Thank you. There's a lot you can do with a wall. People don't know.

Athena   It can't hit back.

Mary Wallace (*suspicious*)   That's true.

Athena   I'm here every day. You should come if you want.

Mary Wallace   I don't live in the city.

Athena   Where are you from?

Mary Wallace   Teaneck.

Athena   Take the train!

Mary Wallace   I don't even know you.

Athena   What's your name?

Mary Wallace   Mary Wallace.

Athena   Mary?

Mary Wallace   Mary Wallace.

Athena   Double name? Mary Wallace?

Mary Wallace   Two words, one name. Mary Wallace.

Athena   It's nice to meet you, Mary Wallace. I'm Athena. Now we know each other!

Mary Wallace   You go by your last name?

Athena   It's my Fencing Name.

Mary Wallace   People do that?

Athena   People should.

Mary Wallace   Why Athena?

Athena   Identify with her story, I guess.

Mary Wallace   Why, you have like a messed-up relationship with your dad? Like the myth?

Athena (*it's not funny*)   That's really funny. Just like *the goddess of strategic warfare* and all that.

Mary Wallace   Right.

Athena   Yeah.

Mary Wallace   What's your real name?

Athena   I'm not telling you.

Mary Wallace   Ha ha, *what?*

Athena   It's a mysterious element.

Mary Wallace   That's very strange, my dude!

Athena   Thank you!

Mary Wallace   You're proud of that?

Athena   I have learned to be.

Mary Wallace   So you have a *stage name* for *high school fencing*. Is this whole thing like a practiced eccentricity? Like is this a *studied performance?*

Athena   No! I'm just trying to be comfortable with my limitations. And I think being mysterious is a way of not tipping my hand.

Mary Wallace   There's a lot to unpack here.

Athena   Don't read into it, okay? I'm not into the whole armchair psychoanalysis thing.

Mary Wallace   *You're not?*

Athena   No, I think it makes people sound judgemental and misguided.

Mary Wallace   What do you talk about with your friends if you don't speculate about other people's mental wellbeing?

Athena   I think that's called bullying?

Mary Wallace   I'm not a bully!

Athena   But are you like a quiet girl who's secretly kind of mean?

Mary Wallace   I'm not quiet, you just don't know me.

Athena   But you are kind of mean?

Mary Wallace   I just have friends. Sounds like you don't have friends.

Athena   You *are* mean!

Mary Wallace   I'm just asking a question!

Athena (*America's Next Top Model, joking*)   I didn't come here to make friends.

Mary Wallace   So you don't?

Athena   I'm just living my life.

Mary Wallace   Who do you sit with at lunch?

Athena   I don't eat lunch. I carbo load before practice. One meal a day.

Mary Wallace   Like a *snake*?

Athena   I read about it on Reddit.

Mary Wallace   Oh, suddenly everything is clear.

Athena   There's a lot of good stuff on there!

Mary Wallace (*sardonic*)   Okay so you *love Reddit*, you don't have any friends, you want me to hang out with you . . .

Athena   I want to practice together. I want to get better.

Mary Wallace   I want to get better too. You're here every day?

Athena   'Til ten o'clock.

Mary Wallace *thinks about it.*

Mary Wallace   Do you always *scream* like that? When you win a point?

Athena *thinks.*

Athena   Only if I've earned it.

Mary Wallace *is at the Fencers Club for her first practice session with* **Athena**.

Athena   I eat eggs.

Mary Wallace   I drink protein.

Athena   I watch tapes.

Mary Wallace   I make notes.

Athena   I mentally catalogue my mistakes.

Mary Wallace   I fixate on mine.

Athena   I don't drink soda.

Mary Wallace   I don't vape.

Athena   My dad smokes. *Cigarettes*.

Mary Wallace   I hold my breath when I walk by smokers.

Athena   I inhale secondhand smoke.

Mary Wallace   That's not good for stamina.

Athena   IT'S NOT MY FAULT.

Mary Wallace   I meditate.

Athena   I don't shave.

Mary Wallace   I run every morning.

Athena   I lift.

Mary Wallace   *You lift?*

Athena   Yeah I lift.

Mary Wallace   Maybe I should lift . . .

Athena   I lift.

Mary Wallace   How much do you lift?

Athena   145.

Mary Wallace   That's a ton.

Athena   I'm strong.

Mary Wallace   Are you *naturally* strong?

Athena   Somewhat.

Mary Wallace   I've got pathetic little adductors.

Athena   That's just leg press.

Mary Wallace   Really?

Athena   That's just leg press.

Mary Wallace   Then I will leg press.

Athena   I study on the train.

Mary Wallace   I download my school books as audio files, then I listen to them while I run.

Athena   Hey, that's a good idea.

Mary Wallace   I use a humidifier.

Athena   I use a dehumidifier.

Mary Wallace   I go on my trampoline every day.

Athena   Wait, why?

Mary Wallace   For my quads.

Athena   But you run.

Mary Wallace   Yeah but I like the trampoline.

Athena   What if it rains?

Mary Wallace   I go on the trampoline.

Athena   What if it snows?

Mary Wallace   I go on the trampoline.

Athena   What if there's a pile of snow on top, two feet high?

Mary Wallace   I push the snow off and I go on the trampoline.

Athena   I use a stress ball.

Mary Wallace   I carry around an ergonomic seat.

Athena   I re-wrap the tip of my blade every day.

Mary Wallace   That's just unnecessary.

Athena   It keeps it smooth.

Mary Wallace   I only re-wrap before a competition.

Athena   I do lifts.

Mary Wallace   I do chair.

Athena   I do chair.

They do chair.

Mary Wallace   I take Marine Biology.

Athena   What does that do?

Mary Wallace   It's my passion.

Athena   Oh, that's great.

Mary Wallace   We stare into the sea.

Athena   I take forensics.

Mary Wallace   COOL.

Athena   I wanna be a human rights attorney.

Mary Wallace   I eat complex carbs for lunch.

Athena   I eat Wendy's chili for dinner.

Mary Wallace   Oh, gross.

Athena   I'm not proud of it. It just ends up happening after practice. My dad gets tubs of Wendy's chili and I've subsisted on that for years.

Mary Wallace   I make something I call a 'pizza potato'.

Athena   What is that?

Mary Wallace   You put a potato in the microwave with Babybell cheese and ketchup and then you eat it.

Athena   I make hot cheese spaghetti.

Mary Wallace   What is that?

Athena   It's where you put a string cheese in the microwave and heat it up and then it becomes a stringy puddle and you eat it with a fork.

Mary Wallace   I wear foam in my shoes.

Athena   I do too! I got these shoes with the round backs that are better for advancing, but I got them a little big because I thought I would keep growing. But I was done.

Mary Wallace   So did I! I assumed I was gonna get taller.

Athena   I don't want to be this height forever.

Mary Wallace   Neither do I.

Athena   You could be taller.

Mary Wallace   What do you mean *I could be taller*? I'm done growing.

Athena   It would be great if you were taller.

Mary Wallace   Of course it would be great, but it's not happening.

They squat.

Athena   I wake up at five to lift.

Mary Wallace   I use this alarm clock app that goes off during the optimal part of my REM cycle.

Athena   I can't sleep.

Mary Wallace   I love waking up. I wake up like a princess. Like . . . Hello! It's a wonderful day!

Athena   Garbage trucks go by my window every night just as I'm trying to go to sleep. 'GUUUUHH GUHCHUNK CHUNK CHUNK.' Right under my window.

Mary Wallace   I love waking up when it's snowing out.

Athena   And then I start drifting off and I can hear when people come up the stairwell . . .

Mary Wallace   I love waking up when it's raining, cozy!

Athena   . . . And inevitably, there's some extremely loud man screaming. I can never hear what he's screaming about.

Mary Wallace   Sometimes there's this big, friendly goose that walks around and honks as I'm waking up in my warm bed.

Athena (*switching conversation*)   I do plank.

They switch from squat to plank.

Mary Wallace   Sometimes the smell of cooking bacon wakes me up –

Athena   WE GET IT, MARY WALLACE.

Mary Wallace   Oh my *god*.

Athena   I can't sleep AT ALL, so.

Mary Wallace   Have you / talked to a doctor?

Athena   Yes I've talked to a doctor.

Mary Wallace   You have like insomnia?

Athena   Yeah that's literally what 'not sleeping' means.

Mary Wallace   Isn't insomnia being worried about not going to sleep?

Athena   No it means I can't sleep.

Mary Wallace   That's impossible. Not sleeping at all? It's not possible.

Athena   Yes it is!

Mary Wallace   Your sleep *quality* could be bad, but you *are* sleeping.

Athena   Why are you being so annoying about this?

Mary Wallace   What you're saying isn't factually accurate!

Athena   It's obviously something that sucks a lot, why can't you just say, 'That sucks.' And move on?

They struggle, struggle, struggle through plank.

Mary Wallace   I'm sorry.

Athena   Thank you.

Mary Wallace   I like winning.

Athena   Yeah me too.

Mary Wallace   I LOVE TO WIN.

Athena   I love knowing for a moment that I'm objectively better than someone else. I spend so much time comparing myself to other people and when I win I can rest in the bliss of knowing that I am truly better, even if it's at this weird archaic sport. Maybe that's why sports exist?

Mary Wallace   I don't think so, I think sports exist so our bones don't disintegrate. And to create a sense of camaraderie. To deal with failure with grace. To sharpen the mind's connection to the body.

Athena   See! Now I feel like you're a better person than I am!

Mary Wallace   I probably am! You take out your frustration by bumping into random people on the street.

Athena   Don't judge me for that, I told you that with care!

Mary Wallace   I'm just reflecting back at you what you've told me.

Athena   You think I'm a bad person?

Mary Wallace   No, but I'm worried you just want to fence me because I'm not as good as you.

Athena   WHOA that's not true at all.

Mary Wallace   Maybe you feel like you're helping me? That makes you feel good?

Athena   I think you're really good! You're helping me!

Mary Wallace   OR – because I'm not as good as you, practicing with me will provide you with validation, and neither of us will improve but your confidence will spike so you'll feel better?

Athena   That is so cynical!

Mary Wallace   Sorry, this is where my mind goes.

Athena   Maybe *you're* not as good a person because that's where your mind goes.

Mary Wallace   Maybe! I don't know!

Athena   I'm not *using you to bolster my ego* or something.

Mary Wallace   Was that weird?

Athena   It wasn't weird, you just don't know me.

Mary Wallace   This is just kind of a socially stressful situation to be in.

Athena   Am I stressing you out?

Mary Wallace   I just don't know what I'm supposed to be doing. Do we talk the whole time?

Athena   You don't have to stress about that.

Mary Wallace   The wall was easier.

Athena   Well, right. I'm not a wall.

Mary Wallace   Right.

Athena   So . . . Are you gonna keep coming here?

Mary Wallace *thinks*.

Mary Wallace   I'm just worried we would become friends?

Athena   So?

Mary Wallace   We're gonna constantly come up against each other?

Athena   Maybe.

Mary Wallace   Definitely. That's . . . Fraught!

Athena   I don't see another way.

Mary Wallace   It's also a long commute. From school, to home, to here, to home.

Athena   Come straight from school.

Mary Wallace   I'd spend so much of my life commuting.

Athena   You will for the rest of your life, why not start junior year?

Mary Wallace   I'd have to ask my parents if I'm going to make this a regular thing.

Athena   Ask your parents.

Mary Wallace   They'll probably say yes. They trust me a lot.

Athena   It's not a big deal if they say no or if you don't want to. I can ask someone else.

Mary Wallace   No, don't ask someone else. Let me ask them.

Athena   When do you think you'll know by?

Mary Wallace   . . . When I ask them.

Athena   Which is when?

Mary Wallace   Tonight.

Athena   Okay, so I'll hold off on asking anyone until tonight.

Mary Wallace   Are you actually going to ask someone else to be your partner between tonight and tomorrow?

Athena   Yeah, I don't know. If something comes up . . . I mean there are a lot of fencers here.

Mary Wallace   Okay, let's just say yes. Let's just say yes, but you have to tell me your actual name.

Athena   Why!?

Mary Wallace   Because my dad was like, 'WHAT'S HER LAST NAME?'

Athena   Come ON.

Mary Wallace   I told him that's your whole name. And he was like, 'Just Athena? Like Cher?' And I was like, 'Yeah, like Cher.' And he was like, 'Yeah, you're seventeen years old, if you wanted to hang out with Cher I would ask her last name too.'

Athena   I promise you he would not do that.

Mary Wallace   Let me disabuse you of that notion. He almost didn't let me come.

Athena   That's ridiculous!

Mary Wallace   What if the last place they knew I went was to practice with a girl named 'Athena' with no last name?

Athena   They'd figure it out.

Mary Wallace   Just tell me your real name!

Athena   I like having a mythical context!

Mary Wallace   I don't understand that, and my parents definitely don't either.

Athena   Make up a name!

Mary Wallace   I don't lie to my parents.

Athena   That's what being an adult is! Successfully learning how to deceive your providers!

Mary Wallace   I'm sorry, I'm close with them. You can ask someone else if that's easier.

Athena   I don't want to ask someone else.

Mary Wallace   I don't want you to either.

Athena   It's not some crazy thing. It's like a wrestler or a racehorse.

Mary Wallace   I hear you. I know how you feel. I wish I was courageous enough to call myself whatever I wanted.

Athena   What would you call yourself?

Mary Wallace   I can't pull stuff like that off. My whole goal is for people to encounter me and be like, 'She seems normal.' And move on. That's all I want. And I get that that's not who you are. But if you tell me your real name, I will never say it. I will put it out of my mind once I communicate it to my parents. It's just something I need to know so we can keep doing this.

Athena   If I tell you, you have to come here every day.

Mary Wallace   I wanna do that. I wanna get better.

A new day – they're sparring, **Mary Wallace** *attacks,* **Athena** *parries, pushes her back no problem.* **Mary Wallace** *attacks again,* **Athena** *parries,* **Athena** *WHACKS her on the upper arm –* **Mary Wallace** *yelps – and* **Athena** *lunges, hits and scores.* **Athena's** *buzzer and light go off.* **Mary Wallace** *flicks off her helmet.*

Mary Wallace   OW.

Athena *keeps her mask on.*

Athena   I can do that.

Mary Wallace   OW. OUCH.

Athena   I didn't do anything wrong.

Mary Wallace   That is so rude!

Athena   No, it's a legitimate move.

Mary Wallace   Says who?

Athena   The judge at Nationals last year.

Mary Wallace   What precedent is there for that?

Athena   It's kind of *my move*.

Mary Wallace   *It hurts.*

Athena   Someone else did it to me, that's how I learned it. But they did it by mistake.

Mary Wallace   So you're just passing along your trauma?

Athena   Can we keep going?

Mary Wallace   Gimme a sec.

Athena   The clock is going and I'm up so I don't care.

Mary Wallace   The clock is not going!

Athena   I'm just trying to be *courteous*.

Mary Wallace   The clock is still going?

Athena   Yeah, cause I didn't break any rules? The clock is still going.

Mary Wallace   Oh my *god*.

En garde, **Athena** *attacks, parry here, parry there,* **Athena** *WHACKS* **Mary Wallace**'s *arm,* **Mary Wallace** *yelps, drops her blade,* **Athena** *scores.*

Mary Wallace   WHAT IS WRONG WITH YOU?

Athena   IT'S ALLOWED.

Mary Wallace   STOP THE CLOCK.

Mary Wallace *pulls off her mask and jacket to look at her arm.*

IT STINGS. YOU FREAK.

Athena   Your chest protector doesn't have boobs in it.

Athena *slides off her jacket to show her protector.*

Mine has boobs built into it. Where do my boobs go in *that*?

Mary Wallace   The plastic boobs just slow you down. They just guide someone's blade right to a hit. It's like having the bumpers up in bowling.

Athena (*thinking about it*)   You're right . . .

Mary Wallace   Yeah. These? Made for a *little boy*. Just slides right off. You should get one.

Athena   Where did you even get that?

Mary Wallace   Craigslist.

Athena   Really?

Mary Wallace   From some Little Lord Fauntleroy in Montclair who decided to take up crew instead.

Athena   I like my weird pokey boob armor. It makes me feel like Wonder Woman.

Mary Wallace   I mean Wonder Woman was an Amazon, so it's not like she would have boobs anyway.

Athena   Why not?

Mary Wallace   The Amazons cut them off so they could do archery better.

Athena   How do you know this?

Mary Wallace   Some book. The name – a-mazos, it means *without breasts*.

Athena   Is that Greek?

Mary Wallace   Classical Greek or whatever. It's very metal.

Athena   You like metal?

Mary Wallace   Yes.

Athena   Oh. My ex ex liked that.

Mary Wallace   What's an ex ex?

Athena   Like the guy I dated before my ex boyfriend.

Mary Wallace   I didn't know you said that, I thought that was still just an ex.

Athena   I dunno, I guess I feel like being pedantic is sort of neutralizing.

Mary Wallace   Fun.

Another day. They're wrapping their blades.

Athena   Do you want to play questions?

Mary Wallace   What is that?

Athena   You just ask each other questions.

Mary Wallace   That's it?

Athena   Yeah.

Mary Wallace   That's all there is to the game 'questions' – you just ask questions?

Athena   Yeah.

Mary Wallace   That's such a low bar for what a game is.

Athena   It's fun! You get to ask really probing horrible questions and the other person has to answer.

Mary Wallace   Are you one of those people who saw *Princess Bride* and decided you wanted to fence?

Athena   Are you playing the game?

Mary Wallace   No, I'm trying to change the topic.

Athena   Fine. Okay, no I've never seen that movie. But I do like watching *Game of Thrones*.

Mary Wallace   Bleh. I think it's unwatchable.

Athena   Oh, so you don't like badass women getting what they want?

Mary Wallace   Most of the women on that show are terribly abused.

Athena   Um, Khaleesi?

Mary Wallace   Um, I guess it just seems like nepotism to me . . . You know? People getting what they want when they were born into a line of power seems easy I guess regardless of gender? I dunno. This language makes my skin crawl. It reminds me of tote bags with trite sayings and all the sad little ephemera of meaningless effort.

Athena (*flinging her weapon around*)   What about Arya Stark?!

Mary Wallace   I actually feel like that character is the bigotry of low expectations personified.

Athena   I don't even know what that means. Like I'm puzzling through that.

Mary Wallace   It's self-evident. You'll figure it out.

Athena *hides her shame in a facial cloak of bemused vagueness: a misbegotten teenage feminist, she wiles the moment off with a flick of her pony. En garde.* **Athena** *fakes* **Mary Wallace** *out, goes low, high, lunges, retreats,* **Mary Wallace** *attacks,* **Athena** *parries, comes back at her hard, hits. Buzzer, light for* **Athena***.*

Athena   I think you're reading too much about feminism stuff and your head has gotten stuck in your own butt or something. Maybe you're spending too much time online? I feel like you're not forming your own opinions. It's like you're being overcome by some amorphous cloud of nonsense.

Mary Wallace   These are my thoughts!

Athena   You sound like walking clickbait. I can feel good about something. Those articles are written to make you mad. Trust me. I know about this stuff from my dad. The only way media makes money anymore is by harvesting your pain, and they're more than happy to make up new ways for you to feel bad about yourself. It's the oldest trick in the book. My advice: just watch public access and read fiction and form your own opinions. I love watching Arya. I get a gut feeling, I feel hopeful. That's my truth.

Mary Wallace   Maybe my truth *is me having my head up my butt*. Wandering around like that. Analyzing everything through my own perspective because that's the one I have. Maybe you can go so far up your own butt you come out your own head. You can't really gain perspective, you can just get more of the same. The ouroboros. And maybe that's . . . Who I am . . . Who I am becoming.

Athena   . . . We're getting along really well.

Mary Wallace   What?

Athena   We are. We're getting along really well.

Mary Wallace   Who says that?

Athena   We're like, speeding right along at a nice clip.

Mary Wallace   I guess it would just be cool if you didn't say that.

Athena   You were thinking it.

Mary Wallace   I was thinking you have terrible taste.

Athena   I don't have terrible taste. I have *no* taste.

Mary Wallace   Oh come on.

Athena   It's true. I don't like music. In general. It's embarrassing.

Mary Wallace   You're from New York City.

Athena   What does that have to do with anything?

Mary Wallace   You're culturally oversaturated so you think it's fun and cool to not have taste.

Athena   This is me, baby! Ha ha, no but really, this is uh, this is the real me.

Mary Wallace   Music is *embarrassing*?

Athena   Absolutely!

Mary Wallace   What does that even mean?

Athena   Like one note folds and dips into the other, it's so intimate and gross.

Mary Wallace   What!

Athena   I don't even like things like doorbells or long subway slowdowns, like 'eeEEEEEE' – the musicality is just . . . A LOT.

Mary Wallace   That's nonsense.

Athena   I'm not trying to be antagonistic, I just – I go to someone's house, they put on music – it's like *okay, we're in a mood now*.

Mary Wallace   I always put on music.

Athena   That's normal.

Mary Wallace   Can you like . . . Not sing or something?

Athena   You think I have a grudge?

Mary Wallace   Uh huh.

Athena   Against music?

Mary Wallace   Do you play an instrument?

Athena   I've been trying to learn guitar for like ten years.

Mary Wallace   And?

Athena   The strings are too close together and my fingers are too big and too short.

Mary Wallace   That's not real.

Athena   It is! My fingers can't go to the places they're supposed to go.

Mary Wallace   Neither can anyone's, that's why there's practice. Did you practice?

Athena   Probably not enough.

Mary Wallace   There you go.

Athena   Okay but I did try and it was clear I didn't have any kind of natural talent.

Mary Wallace   So you give up on things if you're not immediately good at them?

Athena   No, but if it seems like I have no ability whatsoever – that's discouraging, obviously.

Mary Wallace   I hear that fingers thing all the time, but the thing is: hands don't normally do that. It's something you have to learn.

Athena   What do you, like, play classical guitar?

Mary Wallace *looks askance.*

Oh, do you?

Mary Wallace   Yeah, I play classical guitar.

Athena   That's sweet. I love that. I'm very jealous.

Mary Wallace   You hate music.

Athena   But that's not really music, like no one enjoys that, right?

Mary Wallace *chews at the inside of her face, not quite sure if she's justified in feeling hurt.*

Mary Wallace   It can get a bit clinical.

Athena   I mean do you like it?

Mary Wallace *thinks*.

Mary Wallace   I like making my parents happy.

Athena   Is that why you fence?

Mary Wallace   I want to get recruited.

Athena   Me too. Did they sign you up?

Mary Wallace   They thought it would be good for scholarships. And I like running but I'm really slow and can't figure out how to go faster. You don't have to run in fencing.

Athena   Right.

Mary Wallace   How did you get into it?

Athena   Scholarships, same thing. But I got prescribed, initially.

Mary Wallace   De . . . pressed? Anxious?

Athena   Disappointed?

Mary Wallace   Oh.

Athena   The therapist said fencing might be a good way for me to socialize because the sport is a 'self-selecting group of emotionally intense women.'

Mary Wallace   Okay.

Athena   Fencing really helps.

Mary Wallace   What were you disappointed about?

Athena   I don't know. You know? I just wished I was *better*. And my mom moved to Arizona.

Mary Wallace   When did your mom move?

Athena   Oh that's not a big deal.

Mary Wallace   That sounds really hard.

Athena   It's fine.

Mary Wallace   Do you ever talk to her?

Athena   No.

Mary Wallace   Do you want to?

Athena   . . . No.

Mary Wallace *opens the door to her bedroom, and yells down the stairs.*

Mary Wallace   MOM? I LOVE YOU SO MUCH. I'M SO GRATEFUL TO YOU. YOU KNOW THAT? I MEAN, I SHOULD PAY YOU RENT FOR THE NINE MONTHS I LIVED IN YOUR STOMACH, YOU KNOW? AND THEN YOU PUSHED ME OUT OF YOU, THAT'S CRAZY.

Mary Wallace *listens to her mom.*

NO I'M FINE, JUST LIKE I'M VERY GRATEFUL TO YOU FOR YOU KNOW . . . BEING HERE AND GIVING GREAT ADVICE AND GETTING ME ORTHODONTIA BECAUSE YOU KNOW THAT A SMILE IS HOW YOU TELL SOMEONE YOU'RE LISTENING, AND FOR MAKING ME GO TO THE FENCERS CLUB . . . AND FOR JUST BEING HERE.

Mary Wallace *listens to her mom.*

NO DON'T LOCK THE DOOR I'M GONNA GO OUT ON THE TRAMP.

Mary Wallace *listens.*

I KNOW IT'S DARK OUT I'M CAREFUL! I'LL BE CAREFUL!

Athena *is in her apartment, yelling through the door of her bedroom.*

Athena   IT'S GROSS WHEN YOU SMOKE IN HERE OKAY, DAD? I'M TRAINING FOR THE NATIONALS AND I HAVE ASTHMA THAT'S FINALLY UNDER CONTROL AND I'M JUST SAYING IT'D BE COOL,

OKAY, IT'D ACTUALLY BE COOL IF YOU DIDN'T
SMOKE INSIDE. JUST LIKE GO ON THE SIDEWALK
AND SMOKE, THAT WOULD ACTUALLY BE SO GREAT,
OKAY. LIKE THAT WOULD BE REALLY, REALLY
CONSIDERATE.

She listens to her dad.

I UNDERSTAND THAT YOU HAVE A DEADLINE,
FATHER, I HAVE DEADLINES EVERY SINGLE DAY.
THEY'RE CALLED PAPERS, THEY'RE CALLED TESTS,
OKAY? I UNDERSTAND THE CONCEPT, I GRASP IT.
I'M NOT SPEWING A SUBSTANCE INTO THE AIR
THAT TRIGGERS A MESSED-UP REACTION FROM
THE PERSON WHO LIVES WITH ME WHO HAPPENS
TO BE MY DAUGHTER.

She listens to her dad.

YEAH IT'S YOUR APARTMENT. IT'S YOUR
APARTMENT AND I'M VERY LUCKY TO BE LIVING
HERE BUT IT'S NOT MY FAULT YOU FORGOT TO
WEAR A CONDOM AND I SHOT OUT OF YOU OKAY?
THAT'S NOT MY FAULT. I LIVE HERE TOO. DEAL
WITH IT.

She listens, he changes his tone.

WHAT KIND?

She listens.

MAC AND CHEESE SOUNDS GOOD.

They are sparring. **Athena** *WHACKS* **Mary Wallace** *on the arm,*
Mary Wallace *drops blade,* **Athena***'s buzzer goes off.*

Mary Wallace   You can't do that anymore if you want to
practice together.

Athena   Why not?

Mary Wallace   It. Hurts.

Athena   That's the name of the game, baby.

Mary Wallace   Stop it!

Athena   That's not fair! It's a part of my technique.

Mary Wallace   Then take it off the table.

Athena   Imagine if I told you that you couldn't parry. How would you be able to isolate and remove a central part of your strategy?

Mary Wallace   If I knew it was actively hurting people, it wouldn't be that hard.

Athena   This sport doesn't *feel good*.

Mary Wallace   I know.

Athena   I don't know if your parents told you that when they signed you up.

Mary Wallace   It shouldn't have to hurt more than it needs to.

Athena   It doesn't! It hurts just as much as it needs to be effective.

Mary Wallace   No one else does that as a move.

Athena   That's because it's brand new.

Mary Wallace   I'm a postmodernist. I don't think anything is new. Especially not moves in a five-hundred-year-old sport.

Athena   The flick. The Chamley-Watson.

Mary Wallace   Made impossible by technology, and banned, respectively.

Athena   There are others.

Mary Wallace   Name them.

Athena   The ref let me do it!

Mary Wallace   *What exactly happened?*

Athena   I slashed her. She dropped her blade. I scored. The ref gave me the point.

Mary Wallace   And that's all?

Athena   That's all.

Mary Wallace   The ref didn't ask you not to do that?

Athena   No.

Mary Wallace   Did he ask any questions?

Athena   Well he was like, 'What was that?' Because he'd never seen it before.

Mary Wallace   And what did you say?

Athena   Well obviously I wasn't like, 'That's my signature move.' Because I'm humble.

Mary Wallace   So what did you say?

Athena   I don't know. I explained

Mary Wallace   How did you explain?

Athena   I said it was a missed attack or something.

Mary Wallace   OKAY.

Athena   I mean in the moment, it was.

Mary Wallace   I think you're just planning on using this strategy and saying that 'Nationals let you' until you're in front of a ref and instant playback, when you'll drop it cause it's too risky. So why don't you play me like I'm at the top?

Athena   What an INTRIGUING THEORY, Mary Wallace.

Mary Wallace   ALSO I want my fighting arm intact! And my reputation.

Athena   What does *that* mean?

Mary Wallace   I mean I like to keep myself on good standing with everyone. I don't slash at people with unnecessary force. And I don't want to be associated with someone who does.

Athena   So this is about wanting to look good?

Mary Wallace   Are you trying to hurt me?

Athena   What?!

Mary Wallace   It feels like that.

Athena   Hurt you?! Why?

Mary Wallace   I don't know. The goose?

Athena   Goose?! What? What goose?!

Mary Wallace *sighs*.

Mary Wallace   I'm sorry. I do try to look good, look like my life is really nice, and I try to be positive. Sometimes I get a little wrapped up in it, turns me into a big jerk. I can feel myself doing it. It's hard to stop. Believe me, I'm aware of it. It's not so fun to be in my head.

Athena   You think I'm using my move because I'm jealous that you live in like a Thomas Kinkade painting?

Mary Wallace   There's a specific energy to it. It feels personal.

Athena   That would be psycho shit. You don't even believe that. You wouldn't still be here if you believed that.

Mary Wallace   You haven't really answered me.

Athena   I'm not trying to hurt you. I'm trying to get us to push each other. You know? Use every tool we have. Push push push. Have it be . . . Intense, you know? I'm not jealous of your babbling brook, Mary Wallace, I live in the greatest city in the world!

Mary Wallace   Do you hear the words you're using? The verbs? 'Push push push.' I don't want to be pushed! I don't want to feel punished!

Athena   But that's how training works?

Mary Wallace   What did you do, watch *Whiplash* and come out of it thinking the music teacher had a good thing going?

Athena   You're welcome to try it!

Mary Wallace   Practice is how people get better, not practice under duress!

Athena   Why won't you do it?

Mary Wallace   Because I don't want to!

Athena   Just fucking hit me! Just do it!

Mary Wallace   No!

Athena   Because you're such a *good girl*?

Mary Wallace   Yeah, that's the thing about good girls. You can't tell them what to do!

Athena *stops, thinks. Frowns. Nods. Puts her mask back on.*

Athena   I respect that.

Mary Wallace   Okayyy . . . You mean . . . You're not gonna do the move anymore?

Athena   . . . Yyyeah. Yeah. I'm gonna . . . Take it off the table.

Mary Wallace   Thank you.

A shift. **Mary Wallace** *fakes, fakes, double steps, lunges: hits.*

Athena   What are you doing after this?

Mary Wallace   What?

Athena   In the city. What are you doing after this, Teaneck?

'Hearts on Fire' by Cut Copy comes on. **Mary Wallace** *and* **Athena** *are raving in a basement in downtown Manhattan. They are yelling over the music.*

Athena   My sister's the DJ.

Mary Wallace   That's so cool!

Athena   She sucks. I'm wearing her clothes. I hope she doesn't see me.

Mary Wallace   I thought you hated music.

Athena   Sure but I love the vibe.

Mary Wallace   You love the VIBE!? What are you, thirty-six years old?

Athena   Oh my god, back off!

Mary Wallace   I think someone stepped on my toe. I think it's ruined.

Athena   Don't be classist – this is general admission.

Mary Wallace   I've never been to a concert before.

Athena   It's not a concert.

Mary Wallace   I could pretend to know what I'm doing for you but I'm not gonna do that.

Athena   We were lucky they didn't card.

Mary Wallace   You only have a card because of your sister. People with older siblings have an unfair advantage in terms of everything.

Athena   You don't have siblings?

Mary Wallace   No I do, my brother's ten years older. Henry.

Athena   What!

Mary Wallace   He doesn't count, he's a virgin and he's a Libertarian.

Athena   How do you know he's a virgin?

Mary Wallace   He told me.

Athena   Oh gross.

Mary Wallace   We talk about stuff!

Athena   My sister is so mean. She once told me I'm plain.

Mary Wallace   What?

Athena   She said I'm *plain*.

Mary Wallace   What!?

Athena   Plain. Like – nothing. Like my body and face is nothing.

Mary Wallace   That's terrible.

Athena   I love her though, I mean she's so fun.

They dance.

Mary Wallace   I'm not wearing the right thing.

Athena   No one's ever wearing the right thing in New York.

Mary Wallace   Where do people get these clothes?

Athena   Who cares. Fashion is like an arms race.

Mary Wallace   I should catch the bus back.

Athena   Aren't you having fun?

Mary Wallace   I'm having so much fun! I'm just a little dizzy, maybe, from the gin?

Athena   If you're having fun, you should keep having fun! You know my sister? She was hit in the head by a random guy. From behind, with a brick. Just walking down the street. Now she can't remember the alphabet, so she's a DJ. Could happen anytime. You know? You should appreciate life.

Mary Wallace *bounces around, thinking about this story.*

Mary Wallace   I mean tomorrow is Friday, which is basically the weekend. And I have perfect attendance so I could 'be sick' I guess.

Athena and **Mary Wallace** *drink gin out of a Nalgene.*

We're in a hospital, machines beep. **Mary Wallace** *is unconscious.*
Athena *finds* **Mary Wallace***'s phone, uses* **Mary Wallace***'s thumb
to unlock it, scrolls through the phone and calls a number.*

Athena   Hi Henry? No – it's not Mary Wallace, this is her
friend –

She listens.

Not exactly, she has um, food poisoning?

She listens.

I mean a little, we had a couple, um, sips of alcohol, but
that's not –

She listens.

Mount Sinai.

She listens.

My name? Uh –

She hangs up. **Athena** *looks at the phone. She grabs her stuff and
leaves, abandoning* **Mary Wallace** *at the hospital.*

We're at the Fencers Club.

Athena   I am so sorry.

Mary Wallace   Why did you call Henry?

Athena   You don't have 'Mom' or 'Dad' listed in your
phone!

Mary Wallace   I'm an adult. They're listed as Corrinne
and Ben.

Athena   I shouldn't have left you.

Mary Wallace   You took me there. You did the right thing.

Athena   I got nervous. Your brother is like . . . Really
intense. Like, he says the word 'liability' a LOT.

Mary Wallace   That's Henry.

Athena I'm so sorry. I just thought we could have drinks and open up and talk about our thoughts and stuff.

Mary Wallace That sounds great! And I totally overdid it and messed it all up.

Athena No, I feel like I weirdly pressured you.

Mary Wallace You didn't. It was my fault.

Athena Had you ever gone out drinking before?

Mary Wallace My grandma once legitimately spiked my eggnog.

Athena Oh no, I thought you were – you seem cool.

Mary Wallace I'm not. I'm really not. But I did want to try and I should have told you.

Athena You have so many friends.

Mary Wallace We like . . . Play Codenames and eat chips.

Athena I would have said to pace yourself more. I would have made you drink water.

Mary Wallace It could have been really great.

Athena You said you weren't going to pretend.

Mary Wallace I *thought* I knew what I was doing. How hard can drinking be? You just drink!

Athena Are you in trouble?

Mary Wallace I got grounded.

Athena Dammnit.

Mary Wallace Somewhat permanently.

Athena (*at least*) They let you come back.

Mary Wallace I can't um . . . Hang out anymore. Afterwards. Obviously.

Athena   . . . Right . . . Grounded. That's so suburban. I don't think my dad could enforce that if he wanted to.

Mary Wallace   Yeah I just do homework, and go to school, and come here.

Athena   What else could you need?

Mary Wallace *and* **Athena** *salute and go en garde.* **Mary Wallace** *advances,* **Athena** *holds her ground.*

Mary Wallace *hops forward, makes a false start, loops around* **Athena***'s blade, lunges and makes contact with* **Athena***'s collar bone.*

Mary Wallace*'s green light goes off.*

Mary Wallace   Are you going easy on me?

Athena   No.

Mary Wallace   You were going really slow.

Athena   No I wasn't.

Mary Wallace   You took ten years to parry.

Athena   Rough!

Mary Wallace   Come on. You did it on purpose.

Athena   I'm sorry you feel that way.

Mary Wallace   That's not fair.

Athena   *Who are you to decide?*

Mary Wallace   You can't go easy on me.

Athena   Why would I go easy on you?

Mary Wallace   Because you feel bad that I got in trouble? Because you feel like it was your fault?

Athena   I do feel bad.

Mary Wallace   So you *are* going easy on me!

Athena   I didn't say that!

Mary Wallace   You can't lie to me, I can see with my eyes what's happening.

Athena   Okay.

Mary Wallace   Don't do that again.

Athena   Okay.

Mary Wallace   We need to make an agreement that neither of us will ever go easy on the other one. Okay? Never under any circumstances, no matter what. Okay?

Athena   Okay.

Mary Wallace   Otherwise, what are we even doing here?

Athena   Deal.

Another day.

Athena *makes an aggressive advance, makes contact with* **Mary Wallace***'s gut. Buzzer.* **Athena** *whips off her helmet and screams.* **Athena** *puts her helmet back on. They reposition. They chicken dance, advance, retreat.*

Mary Wallace   You seem homeschooled when you scream like that.

Athena   You can't say that to me.

Mary Wallace   I just did.

Athena   Lots of people do it.

Mary Wallace   Like *weird people*. Like a weird person with no self-awareness does that next to me at qualifiers and I'm like – yikes that girl is *not fun*.

Athena   If you knew you could really scream, like you could really freaking let it out after every point, you'd totally fence better.

Mary Wallace   That doesn't make any sense. The only
thing I'm really thinking about when I'm in a bout is how
I'm gonna win.

Athena *lunges,* **Mary Wallace** *parries,* **Athena** *whips her blade
around* **Mary Wallace***'s,* **Mary Wallace** *pushes* **Athena** *back and
scores at her shoulder. Buzzer.*

Athena   Wouldn't it feel great to scream there?

Mary Wallace   Fencing is literally the most polite sport
there is. I don't think it's right to scream at the person you're
sparring.

Athena   Oh so it's rude?

Mary Wallace   Yeah, so it's rude.

Athena   You can say it's rude to hit you in the arm. I get
that. But I can scream if I want to. I can raise my incentive. I
live in an apartment building. There's no freaking . . . Open
woods with babbling streams that I can scream in. There's
no *goose*. I can scream here.

Mary Wallace   You *are* mad about the goose!

Athena   I'm just saying!

Mary Wallace   I don't go to the woods and scream!

Athena   You have *space*. You could if you wanted to.

Mary Wallace   I know this sounds petty, but when you do
that? It's embarrassing.

Athena   I'm not embarrassed.

Mary Wallace   No, *I'm* embarrassed.

Athena   Why?

Mary Wallace   Sorry, but it really makes me stressed out
that people think we're creepy screamers?

Athena   Who cares?

Mary Wallace   I do.

Athena   It really bums me out that you're that self-conscious.

Mary Wallace   I'm not self-conscious!

Athena   It makes me a better fencer. It makes me better at practicing with you. If you don't want to get better because something I'm doing is embarrassing you in front of a bunch of strangers, yeah that makes you pretty self-conscious. I'm not hurting you. I have this. Let me have this.

Mary Wallace *lets* **Athena** *have that.*

Now, **Mary Wallace** *is doing her homework in her bedroom, listening to 'It Took The Night To Believe' by Sun 0. Her landline rings.* **Mary Wallace** *picks up.*

Mary Wallace   Kerry residence, this is Mary Wallace.

Athena   What's that terrible sound?

Mary Wallace *turns down the music.*

Mary Wallace   *Music.* Hi.

Athena   Yeah, uh hi. Why aren't you here?

Mary Wallace   I have a test.

Athena   Why didn't you tell me?

Mary Wallace   You're fine practicing alone for one day. I gotta go!

Athena   Can you please come?

Mary Wallace (*puppy voice*)   Nancy, fetch!

Mary Wallace *throws a rope toy for the family terrier.*

Athena   Mary Wallace, please?

Mary Wallace (*puppy voice*)   Good job.

Nancy retrieves the dog toy.

Athena   Mary Wallace!

Mary Wallace   I can't! It's *seven o'clock*. I couldn't be there til nine anyway.

Athena   I'll stay.

Mary Wallace   I wouldn't get back until midnight.

Athena   You could stay with me!

Mary Wallace   I'm not allowed!

Athena   Now I feel like *you're* punishing *me*.

Mary Wallace   Isn't there someone there?

Athena   There's no one for me to practice with.

Mary Wallace   What about Shayna or Migdalia?

Athena   Shayna already left, and Migdalia's trying sabre today.

Mary Wallace   Oh, is she switching to sabre?

Athena   She might, she hits me in the mask enough to switch weapons and call it on purpose.

Mary Wallace   That'd be great for us if she did.

Athena   I know, right? ('Hi Mio! No I'm staying for a bit. You can leave my stuff there.')

Mary Wallace   Mio's there?

Athena   Yeah.

Mary Wallace   Maybe she can squeeze you in for a private?

Athena   My dad says we're having 'cash flow problems' so no.

Mary Wallace   What about Jordana and CeeCee?

Athena   They suck! How dare you mention Jordana and CeeCee!

Mary Wallace   Jordana's fine!

Athena   I'm not practicing with some girl who wanted to switch to sabre to be a quote 'big fish in a small pond.'

Mary Wallace   You're such a snob!

Athena   Yes I am!

Mary Wallace   Also CeeCee is not bad.

Athena   She's never come close to scoring a point on me.

Mary Wallace   Not for long. She's getting better.

Athena   Mary Wallace? I'm serious. This is not cool. I need you to be here.

Mary Wallace   I'm always there!

Athena   Yeah but you're not today.

Mary Wallace   I'll be there next week.

Athena   Next week?!

Mary Wallace   I have to babysit tomorrow night.

Athena   What the hell, Mary Wallace? I need you.

Mary Wallace   I promise. I'll be there next week.

They're fencing. **Athena** *advances, advances, scores.* **Athena** *whips off her mask, screams.*

Mary Wallace   Oh my god, what happened to your face?

Athena   It's gross. Don't look at it.

Athena *rubs vaseline on her face.*

Mary Wallace   It looks like it's falling off.

Athena   It is.

Mary Wallace   You look like a health class poster. Are you on meth?

Athena   Uh, close. It's Accutane.

Mary Wallace   What?

Athena   Accutane.

Mary Wallace   Ack-ya-whut?

Athena   ACK-YOU-TANE. Accutane. It's for acne.

Mary Wallace   When did this happen?

Athena   Last week. This is what happens when you miss practice!

Mary Wallace   I'm sorry.

Athena   It's like going through puberty all over again.

Mary Wallace   Did this happen when you went through puberty?

Athena   No, it's just like a horrifying change to my body that I can't control.

Mary Wallace   I don't understand. You don't have acne.

Athena   You have no idea how much makeup I normally wear to hide the freaking volcanic nightmare underneath.

Mary Wallace   You know? I take birth / control for that!

Athena   Yeah I'm already on birth control.

Mary Wallace   Oh.

Athena   So they put me on antibiotics for like weeks and that just . . . destroyed my whole colon area you know? Like my butt.

Mary Wallace   Oh god.

Athena   Yeah and then I got Proactiv which just like, stained all my shirt collars and made my acne even worse.

Mary Wallace   Gross.

Athena   And then, this is a fun story: last week I was on the sidewalk, and this girl in my class Antonia was like, 'Hi!' And hugged me. She's like seven feet tall, and my makeup wiped off all over her puffy vest and I just didn't say anything and was just looking at this like, imprint of my face on her vest during the whole conversation.

Mary Wallace   Like The Shroud of Turin.

Athena   So then I was like . . . This is a bad situation. You know? Give me the good stuff. So they were like you have to be on two forms of birth control because if you get pregnant on this stuff, your babies can look like THIS. And then they showed me these GNARLY BABIES with crazy heads and I was like this stuff is *not messing around*. And now my face is falling off and my lips are falling off but my skin looks TIGHT right? Like NO ACNE.

Mary Wallace   Right, just like, large flakes sloughing off.

Athena   Right? That's my oil glands shrivelling up and dying.

Mary Wallace   Wow.

Athena   It's amazing.

Mary Wallace   My palate expander really tears up the inside of my mouth. Looks terrible in there.

Athena   Huh.

Mary Wallace   So . . . You were on birth control for your skin?

Athena   No it was for sex, but my dermatologist was like, we can tell your dad it's for your skin because it also is!

Mary Wallace   Oh cool. So you, like, you're seeing someone?

Athena   I had sex with a guy on a train. It rocked. And then I was like, I should probably invest in this a little more, get on the pill for the future. But it hasn't really been worth it, I've only done it a couple other times. The train was definitely the best location.

Mary Wallace   *The best location?*

Athena   Don't slut-shame me!

Mary Wallace   Oh, no!

Athena   I'm just kidding.

Mary Wallace   I just mean, I would think a train would be like, the worst location!

Athena   That's why it's the best.

Mary Wallace   I would think, like, *a soft meadow* would be best. Like the warm spot that a deer slept in.

Athena   Whoa.

Mary Wallace   Yeah. I uh. I'd love a relationship.

Athena   Really?

Mary Wallace   Yeah. I just – yeah. I feel like I have a lot of love to give. And I wanna get it too. Like I want to make hand-crafted gifts and go on dates and sneak around.

Athena   I had no idea.

Mary Wallace   I'm a romantic.

Athena   Wow.

Mary Wallace   Are you?

Athena   I'm so busy, you know? I'm so busy. I don't know. People get so weird when they have boyfriends.

Mary Wallace   They do?

Athena   I think it's like basically a kind of psychosis. Like gender psychosis.

Mary Wallace   I don't date men. So, I don't really know.

Athena   That's very smart.

Mary Wallace   That's not *really* what it is.

Athena   But I mean all guys, like my dad even, are just, like *so sexist*. Like it's so global, you know? It's so insidious. It's the air we breathe.

Mary Wallace   Sounds like kind of a generalization.

Athena   A generalization!

Mary Wallace   I think my dad's okay. He gave me *Sister Outsider* for Christmas. This all sounds very second wave to me.

Athena   You don't think the family unit is inherently predatory?

Mary Wallace *sees what's going on and takes her time, going gently.*

Mary Wallace   Did you know trees can stretch out their roots and find their tree family, their distant seed-saplings, and share nutrients with them? Like, since TREES. It goes *back*! I think you can say a lot of things are other things, and that's fine. But I think things can be connected in different ways, it doesn't have to be so linear.

Athena   I like trees. I like the way they smell.

Mary Wallace   It's the phytoncides! Chemical compounds, oils from the leaves, when you smell a tree, it stays with you and helps you fight off sickness. Just by growing and being around.

Another day. They're not fencing. They're practicing footwork back and forth.

Mary Wallace   So Catherine was like, 'You can't be on my Ocean Science Bowl team because you have a *social hesitancy* in your voice.'

Athena   *What does that mean?*

Mary Wallace   Right?

Athena   That's rude.

Mary Wallace   I was like, I know way more about marine life than all of you combined: A. B.! I don't like, I don't get distracted! Catherine *knows* Benny and Charlize haven't even taken chem yet, and I took physics, (I'M SORRY!) as a SOPHOMORE. I'm there for the seismic portion, I've got the bio-ecosystems down, I read Nautilus for fun. I'm like born for this.

Athena   What is her problem?

Mary Wallace   I wonder if it's like that I can't hang out afterwards.

Athena   Are you still grounded?

Mary Wallace   Til after qualifiers. I just want to be on a team so badly. I want to be working together with other people. I'm sorry but I come here and it's just conflict, conflict, conflict. There's no like group effort. I feel *so alone*.

Athena   We're working together!

Mary Wallace   Not really.

Athena   We are! That's why I wanted to hang out more.

Mary Wallace   And that was a disaster.

Athena   That's not my fault!

Mary Wallace (*chuckling*)   Alright.

Athena   How is that my fault?

Mary Wallace   I'm not saying it's your fault, it's obviously not your fault. But you didn't take care of me.

Athena   *Take care of you?*

Mary Wallace   Yes.

Athena   I'm not here to take care of you.

Mary Wallace   That's obvious.

Athena   I didn't think I had to babysit you.

Mary Wallace   That's not what I mean. I mean just, basic, looking out for one another.

Athena   You think you take care of me?

Mary Wallace   I've tried to. In the past. I've tried to take care of your feelings, your wellbeing. But you didn't reciprocate, so I gave up trying.

Athena   I was trying to get to know you better the way I knew how. I'm sorry you got grounded. And I'm sorry that's causing all these problems for you.

Mary Wallace   Yeah they won't even let me practice driving so I can't get my permit.

Athena   Who needs to drive?

Mary Wallace   You live in New York City. Only people with huge dogs or musicians who play like *the harp* drive cars here.

Athena   Right.

Mary Wallace   And I was like, 'The worst part, Catherine? The worst part is that this is like my PASSION. This is like . . . MARINE SCIENCE is I want to DO with my LIFE, you know?'

Athena   Why?

Mary Wallace   Because it's everything! It's where we all came from! We all just gushed up out of the sea! The human embryo has gills! We hiccup because we're starved for water! WHALES ARE SEA DOGS!

Athena   They are?

Mary Wallace   THAT'S WHY EVERYONE LOVES THEM! And CATHERINE is IN MY WAY!

Athena   You don't need them!

Mary Wallace   But I want to be on the team!

Athena *Who cares?* You're in high school! You're obviously better than them. No one's ever going to care about some Ocean Science Bowl you did when you were seventeen. Catherine can take her little power trip right to hell and you can go be the best scientist in the world! You can do anything! You're a fencer!

Mary Wallace *is at the orthodontist's office, with a bite block in her mouth.*

Mary Wallace (*talking to the orthodontist through the bite block*) School is fine. Oh, I don't know yet. I'll figure something out. Um. Maybe. Yeah. Sure. I'm fencing? I'm a fencer? A FENCER. I'M A FENCER, I'M A FENCER!

Athena *and* **Mary Wallace** *are sitting on the ledge of the piste, finishing off power bars.*

Mary Wallace   Your face looks worse.

Athena   It's gonna be so worth it. When do you get your palate expander out?

Mary Wallace   I ask her every time I go in. *I have no idea.*

Athena   I can't imagine what you'd look like without it.

Mary Wallace   Like, really really good probably. Like super *hot* and *good*.

Athena   It's like a part of your face.

Mary Wallace   It makes my chin lower. You know? Lower. I'm worried it'll be that way forever.

Athena   I don't think it will.

Mary Wallace   I've had it for nine years.

Athena   That's insane. I've never heard of such a thing.

Mary Wallace   They just keep expanding and expanding and expanding. Maybe I'll have it for college.

Athena   Do you know where you're applying?

Mary Wallace   Mary Wallace does not *apply*, Mary Wallace gets *recruited*.

Athena   You're very confident.

Mary Wallace   I'm very good!

Athena   . . . My birthday's coming up.

Mary Wallace   When is it?

Athena   Next Saturday.

Mary Wallace   Oh.

Athena   We should do something after qualifiers. You won't be grounded anymore, right?

Mary Wallace   Are you sure you're gonna wanna . . .

Athena   See you after you destroy me?

Mary Wallace   What if you destroy me?

Athena   Yeah duh I'm gonna wanna hang out. Either way.

Mary Wallace   Okay.

Athena   Are you not gonna want to see me?

Mary Wallace   Of course I will! I'm just worried.

Athena   You think you'll be like worked up?

Mary Wallace   Yeah, I dunno . , . I'm not great when I don't win. I've gotten pretty *sulky* after losing.

Athena   Sulky.

Mary Wallace   Yeah but I can be cool.

Athena   Okay.

Mary Wallace   We just both have to qualify.

Athena   We will.

Mary Wallace   We just both have to do extremely well so that we both qualify.

Athena　We'll both get in.

Mary Wallace　I don't know!

Athena　Oh come on, yes you will.

Mary Wallace　I don't think so.

Athena　Migdalia and Shayna are gonna get in. Maybe a couple from MFC, one from FAW *max*, and then us. And then there's gonna be thirty crappy suburban girls, no offense.

Mary Wallace　That's a lot of suburban girls who have to be crappy.

Athena　We're gonna slaughter them.

Mary Wallace　I don't know.

Athena　Say *one girl* from *Bergen County* is *half-decent*, worst case scenario. Shayna's like failing Chemistry, she might not even go to qualifiers.

Mary Wallace　Let's not wish ill upon her.

Athena　WHO ARE YOU? WISH ILL UPON HER? I'm not saying that.

Mary Wallace　No, I know.

Athena　I'm just SAYING.

Mary Wallace　Right right. Yeah. I mean. It would change things.

Athena　You would feel better?

Mary Wallace　Yeah.

Athena　You would hang out?

Mary Wallace　Don't murder her!

Athena　I wouldn't murder her! But I have her number. I could like . . . Text her and be like, 'You know . . . Chemistry junior year . . . That's the difference.'

Mary Wallace   What!

Athena   'For colleges.'

Mary Wallace   No, you wouldn't.

Athena   No, probably not.

Mary Wallace   You're thinking about it!

Athena   I really want you to come!

Mary Wallace   How do you have her number?

Athena   I used to practice with her.

Mary Wallace   Oh.

Athena   She's too good, though, I wasn't improving.

Mary Wallace   What a *secret*.

Athena   Do you feel jealous?

Mary Wallace   Kind of! What are you doing composing a text? Don't send her anything!

Athena   I'm just considering possibilities.

Mary Wallace   Just say like: 'are you going to go Saturday?'

Athena   Really?

Mary Wallace *shrugs.* **Athena** *sends the text. What's happening? She's typing!*

Mary Wallace   She's typing!

Athena   She's always on her freaking phone.

The text goes through.

Mary Wallace   Hm.

Athena   Damn.

Mary Wallace   Say no!

Athena   I think she thinks I want to hang out afterwards though.

Mary Wallace   We shouldn't have said anything.

Athena   Um.

Mary Wallace   Just don't say anything.

Athena   I'm just gonna tell her I am.

Mary Wallace   Why? Just say nothing!

Athena   That's so dumb when people don't respond to a question.

Mary Wallace   No it's not! People get busy!

Athena   No, I always respond. It's gonna be obvious I'm trying to game something.

Mary Wallace   Then just tell her the truth.

Athena *thinks about it for a second.*

Athena   Yeah.

She types, sends a text. They watch the phone. They watch.

Mary Wallace   See? She got busy, and now she's not answering. You could have just not answered.

Athena   She's typing.

The text goes through. **Mary Wallace** *crouches and doesn't look.*

She said, 'Maybe I will see you there.'

Mary Wallace   Okay.

Athena   She didn't want to hang out.

Mary Wallace   Don't be a loser. 'She didn't want to hang out.'

Athena   I know.

Mary Wallace   Now you're all sulky.

Athena   Ugh. Ugh. I can't help it.

Mary Wallace   Now we've piqued her interest! She might actually go now because we sent that.

Athena (*agonizing*)   OH NO.

Mary Wallace   No I just mean, put the fact that she didn't want to hang out in perspective.

Athena   No yeah I get it.

Mary Wallace   Please cheer up. I'm not gonna hit you when you're like this.

Athena   I'M SAD.

Mary Wallace   We can play questions.

Athena   REALLY?

Mary Wallace   One round.

Athena   Do you have a crush on any of your teachers?

Mary Wallace   That was fast!

Athena   It's the best question!

Mary Wallace   I mean! No! I mean. *Mrs Oskarsen*. Yeah. But . . . That's . . . Abstract.

Athena   Yeah?

Mary Wallace   Sure.

Athena   Why?

Mary Wallace   She knows so much about civic history. Like what *is* the Truman Doctrine? I know what it is . . . But like . . . She really knows.

Athena   So . . . What do you picture?

Mary Wallace   I just imagine waiting outside her car. She unlocks her door. She gets in. It's unlocked. I get in the passenger seat. She's like . . . MARY WALLACE. WHAT ARE YOU DOING? And I'm like . . .

She double-raises her eyebrows.

And then it's like . . .

Mary Wallace *smiles and shrugs.*

Athena   What?

Mary Wallace   Nothing I guess. It's just a dream I have. It's just the first part. It's just ever the first part.

Athena   Okay.

Mary Wallace   My turn. Okay. When you said that medication 'messed up your butt' – what does that mean?

Athena   It just means like, every time I poop? It really, really hurts.

Athena *nods, thinking about what that would feel like.*

Mary Wallace (*truly*)   That sucks.

Athena *whips her mask on. It's the qualifiers. They're fencing each other.*

Athena   Shit.

Mary Wallace   It's okay.

Athena   Shit shit shit.

Mary Wallace   It's okay.

Athena   Freaking Shayna.

Mary Wallace   It's not Shayna's fault.

Athena   If she hadn't come we wouldn't be in this, like, *knockout round*.

Mary Wallace   One of us has a *chance* to go – and the other – person. You know. Doesn't.

Athena *doubles over and breathes.*

Athena   Oh my god . . .

Mary Wallace   Hey. I'm not gonna hate you if you win. I'm not gonna hate you if you win and then lose your next round and you don't qualify. I swear, I'm not gonna be mad.

Athena   You get sulky!

Mary Wallace   Forget I said that!

Athena   You're saying this now, but it's gonna be so bad.

Mary Wallace   Look: here are the possibilities. You win, you win the next round, you go to Nationals, you get recruited, you become an environmental rights lawyer.

Athena   I DON'T WANT TO BE A LAWYER I WANNA WORK IN ADVERTISING.

Mary Wallace   You said that once!

Athena   Oh, right that's true.

Mary Wallace   Okay. In that scenario, I lose! I don't go to Nationals. I reconsider my options. You know? I know I'm good. I can send my tape out. I can invite coaches to see me practice. I have a lot of options.

Athena   No one gets recruited that way.

Mary Wallace   Okay, please don't knock my backup strategy.

Athena and **Mary Wallace** *shake and salute. Then, they fence. We watch the entire fifteen-point bout in real time.* **Athena***'s up by five. Then two. Then* **Mary Wallace** *is leading. And then, how did this happen?* **Mary Wallace** *wins. They shake.*

Mary Wallace   What just happened?

Athena   You won.

Mary Wallace   What did you do?

Athena   I did my best. You beat me.

Mary Wallace   Did you go slow?

Athena   *I did not.*

Mary Wallace   You were winning.

Athena   I was.

Mary Wallace   It felt like you gave up.

Athena   I got tired. *It was stamina.*

Mary Wallace   Did you give up because you couldn't do your move?

Athena   *No. You were right!* I would've gotten a penalty.

Mary Wallace   You could have kept fighting, but you stopped. *Why did you do that?*

Athena   I'm sorry I didn't play the way you wanted me to play. I know winning can feel kind of awkward.

Mary Wallace   I know how winning can feel! I'm not scared of my own success. I'm enthralled by my own success.

Athena   Then get used to it.

Mary Wallace   Our first bout? You had this killer instinct. *Where did that go?*

Athena   Where is it supposed to be? We're friends now!

And there it is!

Mary Wallace   I have to fence.

Mary Wallace *exits.* **Athena** *takes off her fencing gear. She watches* **Mary Wallace** *crush Shayna.* **Mary Wallace** *qualifies. She will go to Nationals. She gets a medal. She returns to* **Athena**. *She sits, looking at the medal.*

Mary Wallace   It's a guy on this.

Athena   Oh, yeah.

Mary Wallace   They can't engrave a woman onto these?

Athena   The technology doesn't exist. . . . You're going to Nationals.

Mary Wallace   Yes I am.

Athena   I hope you win.

Mary Wallace   I don't think that's realistic. But I think if I keep training as hard as I have I can do really well.

Athena   So I'll see you Monday?

Mary Wallace *looks at the medal.*

Mary Wallace   I don't think that's a good idea.

Athena*'s heart breaks.*

Athena   I'm gonna start running.

Athena *tries to keep it together.* **Mary Wallace** *touches* **Athena** *in some gentle way, maybe on the shoulder, and offers her a little present.*

Mary Wallace   Um, Happy Birthday.

Athena *opens it, it's a little maple tree sapling.*

Athena   What am I supposed to do with this?

And it's the final round of the Nationals. The lighting is totally new. The strip is outlined with glowing light, and **Athena** *and* **Mary Wallace** *are so brightly lit that it's almost hard to look at.* **Athena** *jumps, attacks,* **Mary Wallace** *parries, counters,* **Athena** *flips her blade, drives her back.* **Mary Wallace** *disengages, retreats.* **Athena** *tries again, advances, attacks.* **Mary Wallace** *attacks,* **Athena** *jumps back,* **Mary Wallace** *misses. Chicken, chicken,* **Athena** *fakes,* **Mary Wallace** *deflects,* **Athena** *attacks,* **Mary Wallace** *parries, flips her blade, counters,* **Athena** *parries, counters,* **Mary Wallace** *parries, counters,* **Athena** *blocks, fakes left, fakes right, attacks over her shoulder,* **Mary Wallace** *parries and backs up, regains her momentum.* **Mary Wallace** *fléches, advancing heel over foot.* **Athena** *blocks left, blocks right, blocks left, blocks right, blocks left.* **Athena** *counters, lunges, misses.* **Mary Wallace** *parries and* *lunges into* **Athena***'s lunge and strikes.* **Mary Wallace***'s victory light blasts throughout. She crouches and screams, her fist curled tight. It's a different scream than* **Athena***'s ever has been.* **Athena** *takes off her mask. But – through some theater magic,* **Athena** *is not* **Athena** *anymore, but a younger and spryer fencer named* **Jamie** *– and we're back at the Fencers Club.*

Jamie   Can you not do that?

Mary Wallace   Excuse me?

Jamie   That's very distracting when you do that. When you scream? I'd love it if you didn't do that.

Mary Wallace   I'm not gonna do that.

Jamie   What?

Mary Wallace   I said I'm not gonna do that. I'm not gonna stop doing it just because it's distracting to you.

Jamie   C'mon, dude. Don't be like that.

Mary Wallace   How is it even distracting? I've already won at that point. Is it distracting to your sense of failure?

Jamie   It is, actually. I'm trying to store what just happened. I'm trying to remember exactly where I went wrong so I can remember it into the future. And your scream just scatters all of these memory pigeons to the sky.

Mary Wallace   It's allowed.

Jamie   Lots of things are allowed, it doesn't make them right.

Mary Wallace   Haven't you ever seen someone scream before?

Jamie   In a bout? Only on TV.

Mary Wallace   Okay. So my theory is, if you wanna get there, you better start behaving like you are there.

Jamie   I've always thought those people looked like such monsters.

Mary Wallace   Would that be so bad?

Jamie   Yeah.

Mary Wallace   If they're monsters? I mean, it works.

Jamie   I'm just saying it makes me not want to fence you, you know? It's not like I dislike the people I'm up against. I respect you. I want us both to do our best. But when you do that, it makes me not want to see you. It makes me scared and it makes me feel like you want me to be scared. It makes me wonder if you're mad at me, it makes me feel like a villain, like I'm so terrible you have to scream when you've sliced off my big leathery tail.

Mary Wallace   That's where you're wrong.

Jamie   You think I don't feel scared?

Mary Wallace   No – I understand that you feel that way, but you shouldn't.

Jamie   Why?

Mary Wallace   I'm not hurting you.

Jamie   That's true.

Mary Wallace   So it's something I get to do. I get to celebrate what I've earned. And I don't care if it offends you.

Jamie *puts her mask back on, tries to get back into game play.*

Mary Wallace   We good?

Jamie   I mean, I still hate it.

Mary Wallace   Then hate it.

End of play.